GW01157607

NIRVANA

BLEACH

by James Adler

PHOTOGRAPHIC CREDITS
© LONDON FEATURES INTERNATIONAL LTD
© PICTORIAL PRESS
© REDFERNS
© RETNA PICTURES
© REX PICTURES

UFO Music Ltd 18 Hanway Street London W1P 9DD England
Telephone: 0171 636 1281   Fax: 0171 636 0738

First published in Great Britain 1997
UFO Music Ltd 18 Hanway Street
London W1P 9DD

The author and publishers have made every effort to contact all copyright holders.
Any who for any reason have not been contacted are invited to write to the publishers
so that a full acknowledgment may be made in subsequent editions of this work.

ISBN 1-873884-96-6

Designed by UFO Music Ltd

Printed in Hong Kong by Everbest Printing Company

NIRVANA

BLEACH

by James Adler

ufo music ltd.
18 Hanway Street London W1P 9DD

CHAPTER ONE

Nirvana are undoubtedly one of the biggest, best loved bands to emerge since rock culture was first established. Yet their first album was recorded for a mere six hundred bucks which they borrowed from a friend. When it was released many dismissed it as just another alternative rock offering, but plenty more had the sense to realise **it was the start of something truly great.**

Back in the mid-eighties Kurt Cobain was a young punk

He began to play guitar after discovering the delights of seventies rock bands like Black Sabbath and Boston through a stoner crowd he met in Montesano, but it was the Sex Pistols who really inspired him.

Along with American underground bands like Flipper and Black Flag, who'd been introduced to him by Buzz Osbourne, a Montesano High School friend who played with local band The Melvins, the Sex Pistols changed Cobain's life and loaded it with musical meaning, and before long, he was recruiting his own band members.

Cobain lived between Montesano with his father, and Aberdeen with his mother, and it was at Aberdeen High School that he met Dale Crover, the drummer with whom he formed Fecal Matter, one of his first ever band ventures. Greg Hokanson played bass, and together the trio recorded a demo which included the song 'Downer'.

It may not have seemed very significant at the time, but 'Downer' was a track which would later crop up on 'Bleach', Nirvana's first album.

Fecal Matter enjoyed a noisy, if brief life, but after the odd support slot with The Melvins, fell apart and Cobain took up with another Aberdeen High student, Chris Novoselic.

9

Novoselic, like Cobain, was a punk who loved Aerosmith and AC/DC. He loved underground stuff as well as bloated seventies rock, and so completely understood where Cobain was coming from as a musician.

Initially this odd couple, the skinny, short blond and the loping gentle giant, concentrated on playing Creedence Clearwater Revival covers. Called The Sellouts, they messed around for a while before finding Aaron Burckhard to help out on drums, thereby changing their name to Skid Row. Burckhard however, was soon ousted by Dale Crover, temporarily on loan from The Melvins, and the new Skid Row recorded their first demo with Jack Endino, who had already produced the Deep Six compilation which showcased the best of the burgeoning local talent.

So impressed was Endino with this bright young band, that he handed their demo to Johnathan Poneman, a local DJ who, together with Bruce Pavitt, a fanzine writer and club promoter, was developing the independent Seattle-based label, Sub Pop.

Poneman was on the look-out for neighbourhood bands. He'd spotted a number of them already, and was beginning to realise that a scene was happening on his doorstep - a scene which needed to be marketed. He arranged to meet Skid Row in a coffee shop, and despite Novoselic's drunken, belligerent display, agreed to sign the band to his label.

By the time Skid Row hit the studio, they'd changed their name to Nirvana, and replaced Grover (who, after all, was only on loan) with Chad Channing, a small hippie from Bainbridge Island. Kurt and Chris had noticed him playing with Tick-Dolly-Row alongside Ben Shepherd, who now plays bass with Soundgarden, and asked him to come and jam with them. He did, and they liked his style, so he was in.

Nirvana's first release on Sub Pop was 'Love Buzz' a cover of a Shocking Blue song, and on the B side was 'Big Cheese'. A mere 1,000 copies were pressed up, making this item very valuable for today's collectors.

15

CHAPTER TWO

RECORDING 'LOVE Buzz' was a turning point for Cobain. Up until this point his bands had been semi-serious hobbies, but when he first heard his single being played on a local radio station he knew that he wanted to make a living from music, and that he wanted to hear more of his songs on the radio. He didn't develop high rise ambitions or anything, he simply wanted to be able to tour and record and afford not to do menial jobs, like cleaning. And the next thing he wanted to do was to record an album.

18

Sub Pop didn't make a habit of releasing albums. They just wanted an EP from Nirvana, but the band were already practising hard for their big release. Without the go ahead from their label, who were feeling the after effects of an expensive Green River cover for the 'Rehab Doll' album, Nirvana booked their studio sessions at Reciprocal Studios in Seattle, and on December 24, 1988, laid down five hours worth of basic tracks for 'Bleach' with Jack Endino. Four days later they played at a party for the 'Sub Pop 200' album, and the next day, they put down another five tracks. More was done on January 24, 1989, and eventually Endino charged them for just 30 hours of his time.

CHAPTER THREE

NO DOUBT about it. 'Bleach' was one hell of a heavyweight. Huge sonic whirls of noise mixed with beautiful melodies and delicate words, it depended on thick, dirty guitars and great big gorgeous songs for its power, aiming low and hitting high with a kiss disguised as a punch. Featuring both Chad Channing and Dale Crover on drums, it really acted as a true representation of where Cobain and Novoselic were headed in the formative years of what was to be a supergroup beyond anyone's imagination.

Channing had been a band member for just six months when 'Bleach' was recorded, and although his style was more basic than Crover's, it fitted in exactly with Nirvana's songs at the time. But two songs, 'Floyd's Barber' and 'Paper Cuts', had been perfected on tape with Crover, so remixes of these were used for the album. While the mixing was underway, all the band members fell ill, and had been given codeine syrup to counteract the sickness. Needless to say, they all got well into the codeine and ended up mixing the album on a very powerful downer.

When a tour was set up to promote 'Bleach', Cobain invited Everman to join Nirvana as a second guitarist. Cobain was relatively inexperienced - he'd only been in bands for a year and a half - so having another player on board seemed like a good idea. Although by this time, it was too late for Everman to contribute anything to 'Bleach', despite the fact that he was given a credit on the sleeve notes.

Money was another problem for Nirvana. In the first place, they had to stump up the recording costs which amounted to the grand old sum of $606.17. As everyone was totally out of pocket, struggling just to make ends meet, they borrowed the money from a friend of Kurt's old buddy, Dylan Carson. The friend was called Jason Everman, and had in fact known Channing for a while, even playing in bands with him occasionally. Everman had saved up a lot of money from his fishing trips in Alaska, and he liked the Nirvana demos, so he donated the cash and started to spend time with them.

24

When a tour was set up to promote 'Bleach', Cobain invited Everman to join Nirvana as a second guitarist. Cobain was relatively inexperienced - he'd only been in bands for a year and a half - so having another player on board seemed like a good idea. Although by this time, it was too late for Everman to contribute anything to 'Bleach', despite the fact that he was given a credit on the sleeve notes.

Sub Pop were also still having financial difficulties, and they too had to borrow money to release 'Bleach'. Before this though, Nirvana, plus Everman, headed out on a West Coast tour for two weeks to build up support prior to their debut appearance in the shops. All of them caught flu in San Francisco, and whilst driving around the city, they noticed posters advising intravenous drug users to "bleach your works" in an HIV awareness campaign. Someone was even giving out bottles of bleach for free. In a bizarre way, bleach took on a huge significance - as if it had become the most valuable substance on earth, according to Johnathan Poneman, and so it became the title for Nirvana's first album.

CHAPTER

FOUR

IN JUNE, 1989, 'Bleach' was released. The reaction?   Good. In some cases, very good. Very good indeed.

In Britain, where 'Bleach' was released on the independent, European based Tupelo label minus the 'Love Buzz' track, most of the rock press were unanimous in their judgment of 'Bleach'. It was hailed as the cream of Sub Pop's crop, and stuck at the top of most people's playlists. Writing for the now defunct *Metal Forces*, Carl Williams enthused over this debut, giving it 95 out of a possible 100. 'Anyone who doesn't like this record has got to be deaf' he announced, likening Nirvana to The Beatles crossed with Mudhoney.

Other reference points he employed included Swedish doom metal band Candlemass, America's psycho-psychedelic noiseniks White Zombie, and, believe it or not, Kylie Minogue (he reckoned Nirvana made fellow Seattle/Sub Pop band Tad sound like the ditzy, diminutive Australian pop queen). '... the best of the lot' he summed up, meaning that 'Bleach' was by far and away the most exciting release from Sub Pop, Glitterhouse and all the other small labels who were simultaneously issuing great big dirty grunge albums.

In *Kerrang!*, Britain's authority on rock music, Chris Watts awarded 'Bleach' a slightly more modest three out of a possible five Ks. '... an album that is quick, imperfect, disgusting, and in places, quite exhausting.' declared Watts, evidently not quite getting it, being more of an industrial goth than a displaced grunge addict. Appreciative of Cobain's vocals, he wasn't too keen on Channing and Crover's drumming, although he liked 'About A Girl', 'Big Cheese','Scoff' and 'Mr Moustache'. Missing the point completely, Watts' summation of Nirvana was 'one hell of a piss-up for beery boys with the added attraction of a musical meteorite'. If Cobain ever read this review, he probably trembled in his sneakers. No disrespect to the mighty *Kerrang!*, but someone who understood a little more about the whole Seattle scene might have made a more suitable reviewer.

31

Writing for inkie weekly *Melody Maker*, Push, more usually a dance critic who now edits *Muzak* magazine, was absolutely gobsmacked by the whole 'Bleach' affair. He declared it to be 'both a mental and a physical bliss', going on to praise Novoselic's bass playing, describing it as a 'sprawling, stalking, sulking monster' no less. 'Swap Meet' is celebrated as a 'leg-up to heaven's window', 'Negative Creep' as 'a faultlessly executed and highly succinct thrash' and the whole is said to be 'Tanked up and over the straight edge. Full throttle into oblivion. Yeah, bleached. Gone.'

Reviewing the Sub Pop version of the album on US import, Edwin Pouncey, otherwise known as genius underground graphic artist, Savage Pencil, awarded 'Bleach' eight out of a possible ten in the *NME*. 'Real rock music should hurt' he decided, before going on to explain just how painful Nirvana were. '...the biggest, baddest sound that Sub Pop have managed to unearth' he wrote, enthusing about an album that, according to him, made 'Mudhoney sound like Genesis'. 'Negative Creep' is described as ' a leash strainer of a song that eventually gets loose and goes on the rampage like a rabid Rottweiler', and the single 'Love Buzz' is 'a magnificent couple of minutes'.

For the American Sub Pop album, 'Love Buzz' had its Looney Tunes cartoon show intro cut down because Bruce Pavitt thought it was too long. Recorded straight from the television, this intro was an expression of Cobain's love of children's music.

He collected children's records and other obscurities, admitting in an interview with Pouncey that his actual rock record collection was in fact, quite minimal.

The now defunct rock weekly *Sounds* recommended 'Bleach' a month before its release date. Writer and musician John Robb (now frontman with up and coming band Gold Blade) anticipated Nirvana's debut album lapped up 'Love Buzz' the single, and primed his readers for the full length experience with a snippet in the paper. An actual review of the record went missing with the *Sounds* archives, but chances are it was good.

And finally Phil Alexander, now editor of *Kerrang!*, gave 'Bleach'
three out of a possible five stars in the also now defunct *Raw*
magazine. Calling the album a 'magnificently cathartic experience'
and a 'cool debut', he thoroughly approved of everything except
'Sifting' and 'Paper Cuts' which he thought 'lost it' by being too long
and not quite as atmospheric as they perhaps would have liked to
have been. Nevertheless, overall, he definitely approved.
Elsewhere, in the Antipodean travellers' UK magazines *Due South* and
Southern Cross, 'Bleach' received warm receptions, meeting with the
hearty applause of M. Bellish and Scarlett Pleasure respectively.
Opinions on 'Bleach' were thus more or less united. The album, despite
a few disgruntled murmurings, was a hit.

CHAPTER
FIVE

LYRICALLY, 'BLEACH' was an interesting insight into the workings of one of the most offbeat, brilliant minds ever to grace rock culture with its songs. Despite his constant disavowals to any lyrical significance whatsoever, Cobain was clearly exorcising some of his feelings about his environment, his upbringing and his general state of mind when he sat down and hurriedly scribbled the words to songs at the very last minute.

He insisted that he never thought or cared about lyrics at all, but his later concern about his position as an anti role model would suggest otherwise. If Cobain mustered such strong feelings about the politics of society, why write rubbish? It simply wouldn't have made sense.

The truth is Cobain never wrote rubbish, Even though he left most of the lyrics to 'Bleach's' songs until the night before the recording sessions, he managed to come up with substantial compositions. Certainly his peers understood and responded to them. Rushing to finish everything at Everman's house where Nirvana were staying prior to recording, Cobain knocked out the beginnings of a legendary rock career.

Part of his style was to keep the lyrics simple, mainly because he had trouble remembering them otherwise. This explains the amount of repetition in Nirvana's songs, but this simplicity is anything but a fault. As reviewers often noticed, it added to the beauty of the band's material.

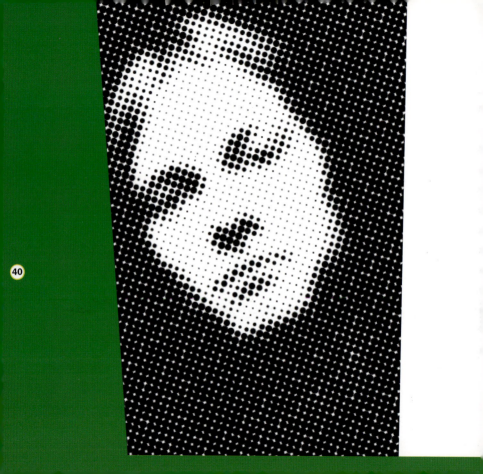

'Bleach' reflects Cobain's perceptions of growing up in the small, redneck climate of Aberdeen. 'Mr Moustache', for example, was about the kind of misogynist often found in smalltown and mid-West America. Apparently, having a moustache was very cool and very metal for high school kids who were into that kind of thing. It denoted the type of person behind it - usually someone who had long hair, wore denim and dealt grass. In addition to having a go at narrow minded macho men, the song makes a dig at the stuck up, condescending politically correct types who frequented Olympia, a small college town in Washington where Cobain lived for a while with his girlfriend, Tracy Marander.

41

Olympia was the home of K Records, a super-PC independent label run by Beat Happening member Calvin Johnson, as well as the alternative arts college, Evergreen State College, and was the headquarters for the riot grrl activity which swept across the States in the nineties.

Cobain had felt stifled by the cliquey atmosphere of Olympia, but when he moved to Seattle he became equally disenchanted by the incestuous music scene. Everything was based around Sub Pop and the bands who were signing to it, as well as the circuit of bars and clubs where everyone hung out. Despite its relaxed, friendly, unpretentious attitude, to Novoselic and Cobain, both longtime misfits, the scene immediately resembled school. Hence the song, 'School', which, Cobain admitted, was written about Sub Pop.

itially meant as a joke song, it
rned out good enough to use on
e album.

ontinuing the anti-social feel of
e album, 'Negative Creep' was
ritten from the point of view of
bad-ass metal type who hangs
round getting stoned all day
nd never bothers to wash their
air. Cobain said he based the
nage on himself, largely
ecause of his highly negative
elf perception.

43

'Swap Meet' as the title suggests, is about swap-meets. Swap-meets happen in car parks, and are basically giant boot sales set up by the working classes of America who don't dwell in large cities. Cobain saw these events as typical of "white trash", and summed up the whole living-amongst-junk mentality with his rather scathing, although empathetic viewpoint.

Tracy Marander was Cobain's girlfriend for several years, and by the time Nirvana came to record 'Bleach', she was beginning to wonder why her boyfriend had never composed a song for her. By now the couple were having difficulties with their relationship because Marander was sick of having to support the out-of-work Cobain. She even warned him that he might find himself homeless if he didn't find a job first. 'About A Girl' details this situation, taking a highly melodic musical direction, and providing Marander with the dedication she had wanted.

'Scoff' and 'Sifting' were both written towards the end of Cobain's crash session in lyrics. He was getting tired and it showed. Both songs have been interpreted by some as biographical, chronicling the way in which Cobain felt neglected both by his parents ('Scoff') and his teachers ('Sifting').

The two songs remixed from the demos recorded with Dale Crover on drums were 'Floyd The Barber' and 'Paper Cuts'. Floyd the Barber was a character from The Andy Griffith Show, an American sitcom which was aired during the first half of the sixties. The song's image of a small town turned rotten, with everyone becoming a murderer, again relays Cobain's claustrophobia at living in a enclosed community.

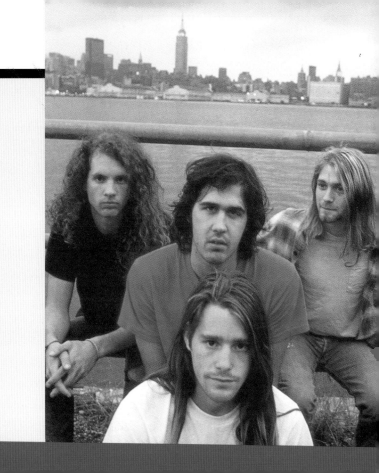

'Paper Cuts' was again, apparently autobiographical. Based on a true story about an Aberdeen family who locked its children up, only opening the doors to feed them and 'clean them out', it also seems to be referring to Cobain's own childhood experiences which left him lacking in love and isolated from his mother emotionally. He felt his mother neglected him, and probably drew some sort of parallel between the physical neglect of the Aberdeen children and his own pain and loneliness.

Finally 'Downer', which was included on the CD version of 'Bleach' only, was a third survivor from the Crover sessions. It was Cobain's politically correct song, written after he became acquainted with PC punk in the vein of Black Flag and the whole underground scene in California.

Looking back on the lyrics, Cobain put them down to naivete, which was hardly surprising considering his later, much more cynical stance.

49

CHAPTER

SIX

'BLEACH' WAS undeniably a rock record. Its production was stripped down and almost stifling, exaggerating the introspective effect produced by the words. At the time, Cobain wanted to make a one-dimensional record, a true rock record devoid of all the later pop which would characterise Nirvana's later releases. He knew what sat well with Sub Pop, and tapered his musical leanings to fit in with the crowd, much as he would draw on his huge pop sensibility for 'Nevermind', and his punk sensibility for 'In Utero'. With this in mind, it's easy to see why Cobain eventually became so disillusioned with music. He spent all of his recording career consciously manipulating his talent to wring the most from whichever market he was aiming for, rather than sticking to his own internal tune. Despite his punk attitude, it was almost a hard and fast, very capitalist method.

He always wanted to please people and gain popularity that way, instead of just throwing his dice on the table and taking a chance. He was very clever, if very cynical, but ultimately, this careful, crafty approach proved to be his downfall.

Not that any of this mattered when Nirvana were busy burning holes in ears with 'Bleach'. Besides, it wasn't as if Cobain denied himself or compromised himself, he simply played the game, combining his rules with those of the business. He loved punk, he loved pop and he loved the rock bands which fuelled the fire for 'Bleach'. In particular, Black Sabbath were big favourites of both Cobain and Novoselic, and the Birmingham heavy metal band's obvious influence on Nirvana helped to make them cool again.

53

CHAPTER
SEVEN

THE ARTWORK for 'Bleach' was a big clue to Nirvana's rock leanings. Hair was very important to the Sub Pop identity - it was one of the things which had attracted Novoselic and Cobain to Everman, who had cascades of corkscrew curls winding down his back. But before a suitable image for the album was decided upon, there were a few obstacles to be overcome.

Initially the band wanted to use a shot Marander had taken of them on stage at the Reko/Muse, a small club which doubled up as an art gallery in Olympia. But Bruce Pavitt had photographer Alice Wheeler in mind, and commissioned her to take individual black and white portraits of the band members. These shots were particularly unflattering, as they'd been taken beneath fluorescent lighting, but Pavitt loved them because they showed the band in all their spotty, un-enhanced glory, and fitted in beautifully with the down-at-home Sub Pop image. The anti-glamour delighted Pavitt, but Cobain thought Wheeler had made him and his bandmates look like mutants.

56

The back cover was originally meant to be a photograph of Everman on stage. Taken by Charles Peterson, the man responsible for giving Sub Pop its strong, instantly recognisable visual identity, the shot was full of movement and hair, but Cobain didn't approve, so the picture was published on a limited edition poster which was packaged with the first 2,000 black vinyl issues of 'Bleach' (the first thousand were to be pressed on white vinyl).

Eventually, everyone agreed on using a negative of a Charles Peterson live shot of Cobain. The hair was there, the movement was there, and the image was a striking one.

CHAPTER EIGHT

IN ORDER to promote 'Bleach', the band had to play live. On June 9th, they appeared at Seattle's Moore Theatre, first on the bill to labelmates Tad, and Sub Pop's most popular signing so far, Mudhoney. The evening went under the monicker, Lamefest '89, and was the biggest Sub Pop event of its time.

Realising their legal situation with their label, Nirvana now demanded a contract from Pavitt and Poneman. Only Soundgarden had been granted an official agreement so far, but while in effect the document was null and void, Nirvana got their piece of paper.

By now 'Bleach' had begun to sell. Its reputation preceded any of the band's dates, and when they embarked on their tour of June 1989 it was zipping out of the shops.

60

The tour took its toll on Nirvana. Taking in a good deal of America, it was a difficult and tiring experience for everyone, and one by one, they all hit the bottle or the medicine cabinet. Hours and hours spent crammed up into a small van hurtling up and down freeways gave everybody road fever, although morale was high. On average, the band were paid one hundred dollars per show, which just about covered their petrol and food expenses, but it was worth it when songs of theirs were aired on college radio stations, and audiences began increasing at the shows.

During Nirvana's first big tour, it became apparent that Everman wasn't quite right for the band. His onstage antics gradually grew more and more embarrassing to the other three, as he strutted about tossing his hair and acting like a big macho metal guy. He'd always been something of a misfit, moody and distant and temperamental, but his penchant for chasing girls was completely out of character for the rest of Nirvana, who either had girlfriends, or simply didn't view girls as rock chick fodder in the way Everman obviously did.

ngs came to a head when Cobain smashed a guitar after a gig and Everman, who was ting the bill because no one else had any ney, got angry.

Everman's final show with Nirvana was at the Pyramid Club in New York during the New Music Seminar, an annual event where lots of new bands showcase their material. The guitarist had become more and more withdrawn, and during Nirvana's stay in New York, he went his own way, hanging out at different gigs to everyone else, leaving himself out of any group socialising and even meals. Eventually, Cobain and Novoselic decided they were going to ask him to quit.

No official announcement was ever made to Everman though. Cobain never enjoyed confrontations, so instead the last seven gigs of the tour were cancelled, and everyone rode home in an awkward silence.

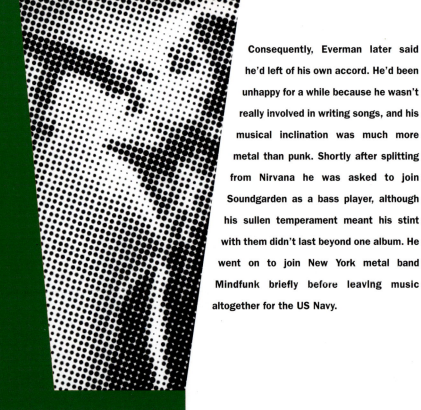

Consequently, Everman later said he'd left of his own accord. He'd been unhappy for a while because he wasn't really involved in writing songs, and his musical inclination was much more metal than punk. Shortly after splitting from Nirvana he was asked to join Soundgarden as a bass player, although his sullen temperament meant his stint with them didn't last beyond one album. He went on to join New York metal band Mindfunk briefly before leaving music altogether for the US Navy.

WITHOUT EVERMAN, Nirvana carried on as a trio, and in the winter of 1989, they travelled to Europe with Mudhoney and Tad with the Lamefest Show. The tour was even harder than the previous one. Food was bad, ill health set in, and although in terms of sales the shows were successful (the two London dates sold out), for Cobain things were already getting out of hand. In Rome he had a nervous breakdown, and declared to his label boss, Johnathan Poneman, who had flown out for some of the dates, that he wanted to quit music and go home to be with Marander. Somehow he kept going for the last two weeks of the tour, with just one gig in Switzerland being cancelled.

CHAPTER
NINE

BY ALL accounts, 'Bleach' had been a success. After the London Lamefest shows it was clear who would end up ruling Sub Pop's roster.

Their rock-driven debut had helped place Nirvana further out than anything else to emerge from Seattle, and while they would change direction completely with their next album, for the time being, Nirvana had won over the underground rock crowds on both sides of the ocean, and laid the groundwork for the biggest explosion of the decade. Looking back at the Nirvana which made 'Bleach', as opposed to the Nirvana which went on to conquer the world, it's difficult to believe that these roughshod kids in grubby flannel shirts and worn-out sneakers would turn into superstars.

Old black and white photos of the band goofing around without a care in the world greater than where the next beer was coming from are hard to reconcile with the troubled, traumatised machine which Cobain ended up driving. And perhaps therein lies the true beauty of 'Bleach' several years on from its original release date. In a strange way it acts as a reminder of a time when Nirvana were untouched by fame, fortune and all the accompanying bloodsuckers. A time when Nirvana were just three ordinary kids from a nowhere town with nothing in their pockets except songs which could move mountains.

IN APRIL 1992, just three years after its initial release date, 'Bleach' was remastered and reissued through Geffen Records, Nirvana's new label. In America, the CD was released with a version of 'Downer' on it, and in Britain, the extra tracks were 'Big Cheese' and 'Downer'.

This time round, Kerrang! awarded the album four out of five stars, with journalist Morat declaring it, quite simply, to be 'very good indeed.'